W9-BYH-245

CODE RED

JANUARY 12, 2010

Earthquake in Haiti

by Miriam Aronin

Consultant: Robert Maguire
Associate Professor of International Affairs
and Director of the Haiti Program
Trinity Washington University, Washington, D.C.

BEARPORT
PUBLISHING

New York, New York

Credits

Cover and Title Page, © Mark Pearson/Alamy; TOC, © Winnipeg Free Press, Thursday, January 14, 2010/ Newspaper Archive; 4, © AP Images/Ramon Espinosa; 5, © Damon Winter/The New York Times/Redux; 6, © James Breeden/Pacific Coast News/Newscom; 7, © Rick Loomis/Los Angeles Times/MCT/Newscom; 8, © Patrick Farrell/Miami Herald/MCT/Newscom; 9, © AP Images/Rodrigo Abd; 10, © Jean-Paul Pelissier/ Reuters/Landov; 11, © Marco Dormino/UN/Minustah/Reuters/Landov; 12, © Lynsey Addario/New York Times/VII Photo Agency LLC; 13T, © U.S. Navy/Mass Communication Specialist 2nd Class Justin Stumberg; 13B, © U.S. Navy/Mass Communication Specialist 2nd Class Daniel Barker; 14, © AP Images/ Bebeto Matthews; 15, © Matthew Bigg/Reuters/Landov; 16L, © Pedro Portal/El Nuevo Herald/MCT/ Newscom; 16R, © Olivier Laban-Mattei/AFP/Newscom; 17, © AP Images/Ramon Espinosa; 18, © Talia Frenkel/American Red Cross; 19, © AP Images/Mark Davis/Hope for Haiti Now; 20, © AP Images/J. Pat Carter; 21, © AP Images/Ariana Cubillos; 22T, © Lui Kit Wong/The News Tribune; 22B, Courtesy of Pamela Bridge; 23T, Courtesy of the British Red Cross; 23B, Special thanks to Ashley Johnson, The Empowerment Academy #262, Baltimore Maryland; 24, © U.S. Navy/Logistics Specialist 1st Class Kelly Chastain; 25, © Pasqual Gorriz/United Nations Photos/AFP/Newscom; 26T, © Hans Deryk/Reuters/Landov; 26BL, © Hazel Trice Edney/NPPA; 26BR, © Lexey Swall/Naples Daily News; 27, © Michael Laughlin/Sun Sentinel/MCT/ Newscom; 28T, © AP Images/Ramon Espinosa; 28B, © AP Images/J. Pat Carter; 29T, © Hans Deryk/ Reuters/Landov; 29C, © Nicholas Kamm/AFP/Newscom; 29B, © Brian Vander Brug/Los Angeles Times/ MCT/Newscom 30, © Winnipeg Free Press, Thursday, January 19, 2010/Newspaper Archive; 31, © Winnipeg Free Press, Thursday, January 15, 2010/Newspaper Archive.

Publisher: Kenn Goin
Editorial Director: Adam Siegel
Creative Director: Spencer Brinker
Design: Dawn Beard Creative
Photo Researcher: Omni-Photo Communications, Inc.

Library of Congress Cataloging-in-Publication Data

Aronin, Miriam.
  Earthquake in Haiti / by Miriam Aronin.
    p. cm. — (Code red)
  Includes bibliographical references and index.
  ISBN-13: 978-1-936088-66-9 (library binding)
  ISBN-10: 1-936088-66-5 (library binding)
  1. Haiti Earthquake, Haiti, 2010—Juvenile literature. I. Title.
  F1928.2.A76 2011
  972.9407'3—dc22

                                     2010011126

For more information, write to Bearport Publishing Company, Inc., 101 Fifth Avenue, Suite 6R, New York, New York 10003. Printed in the United States of America in North Mankato, Minnesota.

072010
042110CGD

10 9 8 7 6 5 4 3 2 1

Contents

Tuesday, January 12, 2010

At 4:53 P.M., Wismond Exantus Jean-Pierre was working in a small grocery store inside the Napoli Hotel in Port-au-Prince (*port*-oh-PRIHNS), Haiti. Suddenly, the earth started to shake. The building began to crumble around him.

Wismond dove under a desk, which protected him from falling **rubble**. His quick action saved his life, but he was now trapped in a small space under the destroyed building.

While he was trapped, Wismond kept up his strength by drinking soda and eating potato chips that he found in the ruined store.

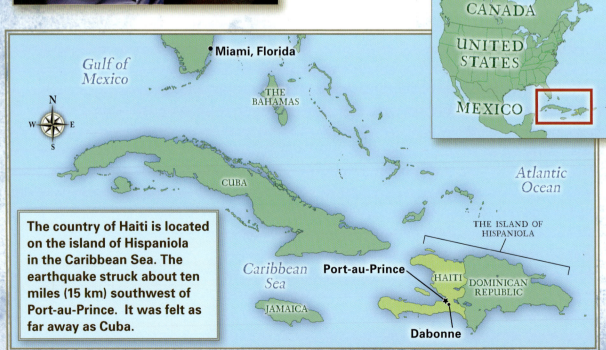

The country of Haiti is located on the island of Hispaniola in the Caribbean Sea. The earthquake struck about ten miles (15 km) southwest of Port-au-Prince. It was felt as far away as Cuba.

4

The shaking that Wismond felt was a massive **earthquake**. It measured 7.0 on the **Richter scale**, equal to the explosive force of several nuclear bombs! In about 40 seconds, the earthquake flattened almost all the buildings in Port-au-Prince.

The area of downtown Port-au-Prince where Wismond was trapped

When the earthquake struck, Port-au-Prince was a busy city. By some estimates, more than 2.5 million people lived in the city and its suburbs. As Haiti's capital, it was also home to the country's government.

"Schools have collapsed. Hospitals have collapsed.... It is a catastrophe.**"**

–René Préval, Haiti's president

Falling Buildings

Many people were killed by the falling buildings. Others were trapped under **debris**, like Wismond. Even people who escaped the buildings often had serious injuries. Many had broken bones, cuts, and burns.

A poor area of Port-au-Prince where many homes were destroyed by the earthquake

Haiti is a very poor country. Before the earthquake, 78 percent of Haitians lived on less than two dollars a day. Many lived in poorly built homes, which could not withstand the earthquake.

American student Christa Brelsford was **volunteering** in Haiti for a program that helps teach people to read. When the earth began shaking, she was inside a house in Dabonne, a town 12 miles (19 km) south of Port-au-Prince. As the building shook, huge pieces of concrete fell onto her legs.

Christa's friend Wenson Georges helped move the concrete off her. Then he carried Christa on a motorcycle to find help. Because she was an American citizen, Christa was **evacuated** to the United States for treatment.

On January 13, Christa waits to be flown to Miami, Florida, for medical treatment.

"My right leg had been almost cut off."

–Christa Brelsford

A Call for Help

Christa was lucky. Many injured earthquake **victims** could not reach medical care. The earthquake had destroyed hospital buildings. Doctors and medical supplies were scarce.

Uninjured **survivors** faced tough times, too. Falling buildings had destroyed food stores and water systems. Rubble blocked the roads.

After the earthquake, Haitians rushed to help the injured and rescue those trapped in ruined buildings. Gladys Louis Jeune, shown here, was rescued after being buried under rubble for 43 hours.

Most survivors were missing friends and family members. They searched through rubble for loved ones trapped underneath. Sadly, many searchers found only lifeless bodies. There were so many bodies that there was nowhere to bury them all. Survivors had to pile the dead in the streets until they could be buried in mass graves.

Many Haitians who lost their homes spent the nights after the earthquake outdoors in parks or on streets.

Terrified survivors felt the earth shake again and again on Tuesday and Wednesday. More than 30 major **aftershocks** hit Haiti after Tuesday's huge earthquake. Each one measured at least 4.5 on the Richter scale.

" Port-au-Prince is devastated. Please help us. "

–E-mail from American health care worker Louise Ivers to friends in the United States

The World Takes Action

Countries around the world quickly answered the calls for help. On January 14, U.S. president Barack Obama promised $100 million for relief efforts. That money would be used for activities such as searching for survivors and **airlifting** water and medicine to people affected by the disaster.

International organizations promised help, too. The day after the earthquake, the United Nations (UN) promised $10 million in emergency money to Haiti. The World Bank planned to give $100 million.

"We stand ready to assist the people of Haiti."

–U.S. president
Barack Obama
on January 14, 2010

This French rescue team prepares to leave for Haiti along with its rescue dog. Many countries, including the United States, China, Iceland, Israel, and Russia, also sent rescuers and medical workers.

10

Meanwhile, **Doctors Without Borders** began setting up treatment centers in tents. There, medical workers would be able to care for injured earthquake victims. Bringing supplies and aid workers into the ruined country took time, however. Many Haitians grew **desperate**—crowding around cars carrying international workers. "They just want help," explained an official from Doctors Without Borders.

By February 25, the United States had sent aid to Haiti worth almost $700 million, including the $100 million President Obama promised right after the quake.

In the days after the earthquake, roads blocked by debris made it difficult for the UN and other organizations to bring enough food for all the hungry people in Haiti.

A Humongous Task

The medical workers and rescuers who came to Haiti faced a **humongous** task. There were tens of thousands of injuries, many of them life-threatening. Even though hundreds of doctors, nurses, **paramedics**, and rescue teams had rushed to the island, still more were needed.

One team of American doctors and nurses worked nonstop for three days and nights. They did operations to save sixty arms and legs. They had to **amputate** another forty. Sadly, they could not save all their patients' lives.

American doctors amputated 12-year-old Mystil Jean Wesmer's destroyed leg.

While doctors cared for the injured, rescuers searched for people trapped in the rubble. On the morning of January 23, eleven days after the earthquake, Haiti's government declared the search over. Anyone buried for that long had little chance of surviving.

This woman was trapped for five days without food or water before she was rescued by members of the Los Angeles County Fire Department.

One of the youngest people rescued was Elisabeth Jossaint. Eight days after the earthquake, rescuers pulled Elisabeth from her family's ruined home. The baby, who was less than one month old, was still in her crib. Amazingly, she was not hurt.

Waiting

As people in Haiti struggled to survive, people around the world waited for news about loved ones. The large Haitian communities in New York City, Florida, and Boston followed details of the disaster closely. Brooklyn fifth-grader Christian Harley, who had family members in Haiti, said "I'm really sad. I don't know what happened to any of my relatives."

Haitian Americans in Brooklyn, New York, prayed and waited for news of their loved ones.

Back in Haiti, Wismond was also waiting—for someone to find him. It was very dark where he was buried. He could not even tell when it was night or day outside.

Wismond had tried to get rescuers' attention. He'd banged against wood and cried out. For more than ten days, no one answered his cries. He began to lose hope.

A boy stares at his ruined neighborhood two months after the quake.

About 230,000 people were killed in the deadly earthquake. Around 1.5 million more lost their homes. One third of all people living in Haiti were severely affected by the disaster.

❝I felt that I had a very slim chance of being found.❞

–Wismond Exantus Jean-Pierre

15

An Incredible Rescue

On January 23, a few hours after the government ended its search for survivors, Wismond's brother, Jean Elit, returned to the hotel where Wismond had been working. For several nights, he'd dreamed that his brother was still alive under the ruins.

Amazingly, at the hotel Jean Elit heard Wismond knocking on a piece of wood and calling out. He immediately ran as fast as he could to find help.

"I'm under the store."

–Wismond, calling out from under the ruins

Crowds of Haitians and reporters watched as rescuers freed Wismond and loaded him into an ambulance. "If they had given up on me, I would not be here today," he said.

By 2:00 P.M., Greek, American, and French rescuers had gathered to free Wismond. They used **radar** to find his location—about 30 feet (9 m) below a pile of concrete and wood. Then, to reach him, they began to dig a tunnel through the debris. After more than two hours, they were finally able to pull Wismond out alive.

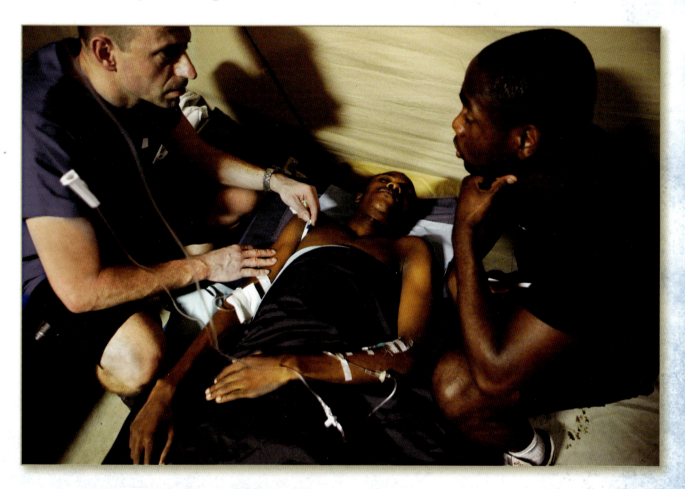

Wismond was rescued 11 days after the big quake. By then, rescuers had saved more than 130 other people from under ruined buildings.

Wismond was treated at this temporary field hospital, run by the French. Thousands of victims were treated at such hospitals during the earthquake's aftermath.

Raising Money

Relief organizations badly needed money to help treat survivors like Wismond. With so many people injured by buildings that collapsed, without adequate supplies of water, food, and medicine, and with many roads blocked by debris— there was enormous need in Haiti. Even though hundreds of millions of dollars had been donated by governments and individuals, the cost of rescuing Haiti would require even more.

An American Red Cross worker helps a Haitian woman with supplies.

On January 22, actor George Clooney and Haitian-born rapper Wyclef Jean organized the Hope for Haiti Now concert to raise money. More than 100 famous actors and musicians took part, performing live in Los Angeles, New York, and Haiti.

Viewers watching the Hope for Haiti Now concert on television sent more than $58 million to relief organizations. That was the most money ever collected during a television **fund-raiser**.

"The Haitian people need our help. They need to know they're not alone."

–George Clooney at the Hope for Haiti Now concert

"A Huge Difference"

By January 24, Americans had raised more than $380 million for Haiti. Christa Brelsford was one of them.

Christa was very grateful to Wenson Georges and other friends in Haiti. She decided she wanted to return their kindness. On the day she left the hospital, Christa announced that she was starting an organization called Christa's Angels.

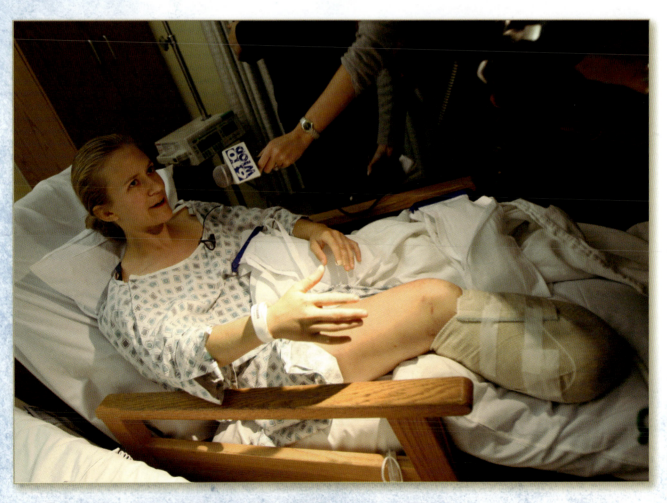

Doctors at Jackson Memorial Hospital in Miami had to amputate her leg, but Christa knew she was lucky to be alive.

66 They saved my life. 99

–Christa Brelsford, talking about her Haitian friends

The organization would raise money to rebuild schools that were destroyed during the earthquake. It would also give Wenson a scholarship to study in the United States. Christa said, "If Americans give a little back, it can make a huge difference."

Hurricane Gustav hit Haiti in 2008.

Haiti has faced many natural disasters in the past. Before 2010, the last major earthquake to hit Port-au-Prince happened in 1770. In 2008, four hurricanes caused huge floods and destroyed bridges. The 2010 earthquake, however, was the most destructive disaster of all.

21

Kids Help Out

Across the world, kids saw news about earthquake survivors. "It made me sad," said nine-year-old Drew Abdella from Pullyaup, Washington. "They had no food, no water, no medicine." Drew's family and friends sold hot chocolate to raise money for Haiti.

Selling hot chocolate for Haiti

Students from Kyrene de la Sierra Elementary School in Arizona raised more than $662 at a lemonade stand. They gave the money to the American Red Cross.

At a school in Daventry, Great Britain, kids made hats to wear in a parade through their town. Citizens watching the parade made **donations** to the British Red Cross for their work in Haiti.

For Valentine's Day, students in Baltimore, Maryland, sold handmade cards. They donated the money to earthquake relief. The students called their fund-raiser "Sending Love to Haiti."

"Hats for Haiti" parade-goer from St. James Infant School in Daventry, Great Britain

Baltimore students made Valentine's Day cards like this one as part of their Sending Love to Haiti fund-raiser.

Rebuilding a Nation

Raising money could not solve all of Haiti's problems. The earthquake had destroyed the country's **economy**. Most survivors had no money and no job. To improve this situation, the United Nations, other organizations, and countries such as the United States set up **cash-for-work** programs. These programs provided jobs and paid wages to survivors to do work such as clearing debris that had blocked roads.

"These young men are doing a little every day to help get our city going again," said the manager of an American cash-for-work program in Port-au-Prince.

The UN's cash-for-work program began on January 27. Within a few days, it was paying 30,000 people to clear rubble. By the end of February, the UN and U.S. cash-for-work programs, along with those created by other organizations, were providing more than 100,000 jobs in Haiti.

Under the UN cash-for-work program, each worker earned $4.50 for working six hours a day.

On February 16, clothing makers in the United States announced a plan that would lead to more jobs in Haiti. They set a goal to have 1 percent of all clothing that they **imported** into the United States to come from Haitian factories.

66 The cash-for-work program is bringing immediate results … to the people of Haiti. 99

–Kim Bolduc, UN official

More to Do

Three weeks after the earthquake, former U.S. president Bill Clinton visited Haiti. After his visit, he wrote, "The long road to recovery has just begun."

Survivors struggled with the pain of having lost loved ones. Patrick Delatour was in charge of **tourism** for Haiti's government. He had lost both of his elderly parents. Frantz Thermilus, a top police official, had lost his 11- and 12-year-old daughters.

"We must all... help Haiti rebuild its future."

—Bill Clinton, former U.S. president and UN special envoy to Haiti

Survivors Patrick Delatour (left) and Frantz Thermilus

Many survivors who had lost their homes were living in tents. They needed new homes before heavy spring rains began in March and the hurricane season, which threatened devastating storms, started in June.

Despite everything, Haitians like Patrick and Frantz hoped to rebuild their country. Luckily, the world would make sure that they and the millions of Haitians who had shown such great courage and strength during their ordeal would now have help.

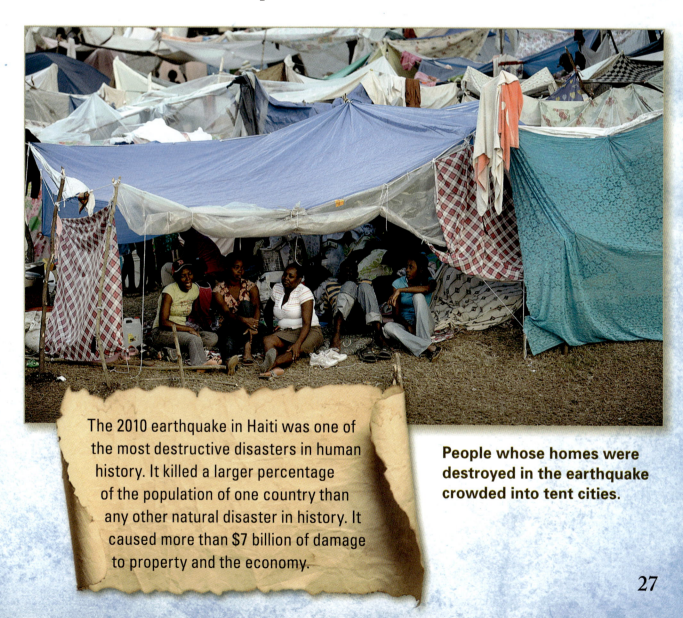

The 2010 earthquake in Haiti was one of the most destructive disasters in human history. It killed a larger percentage of the population of one country than any other natural disaster in history. It caused more than $7 billion of damage to property and the economy.

People whose homes were destroyed in the earthquake crowded into tent cities.

Profiles

Many people showed great courage and compassion in the aftermath of Haiti's 2010 earthquake. Here are four of them.

Wismond Exantus Jean-Pierre was a 24-year-old living in Port-au-Prince.

- Was buried under rubble from a falling building during the earthquake
- Survived by eating snacks and drinking sodas from the grocery store where he was trapped
- Yelled and knocked on wood to help rescuers find him
- Was saved by Greek, French, and American rescuers after being trapped for 11 days and then was taken to a French field hospital

Christa Brelsford was an American volunteer in Haiti.

- Was trapped by falling concrete during the earthquake
- Was saved by friends such as Wenson Georges and brought to the United States for medical care
- Had her right leg amputated because it was badly injured during the earthquake
- Started the charity Christa's Angels to help Haiti and show thanks to her rescuers

Former U.S. president Bill Clinton was the UN special envoy, or messenger, to Haiti.

- Was in charge of raising money and helping deliver UN aid to Haiti
- Visited Haiti twice in the weeks after the earthquake to meet with officials and deliver supplies
- With George W. Bush, another former U.S. president, helped start the Clinton Bush Haiti Fund to raise money for relief

René Préval was the president of Haiti.

- Lost his home when the earthquake destroyed Haiti's presidential palace
- Told the world about the "unimaginable" destruction in his country and asked for help
- Led a national day of mourning for the victims of the earthquake on February 12, 2010

When the earthquake destroyed Haiti's presidential palace, President Préval lost his home. Like thousands of Haitians, he had nowhere to sleep.

Glossary

aftershocks (AF-tur-*shoks*) smaller earthquakes that come shortly after a bigger earthquake in the same area

airlifting (AIR-lift-ing) transporting by airplane or helicopter

amputate (AM-pyoo-*tayt*) to cut off an arm or a leg for medical reasons

cash-for-work (KASH-FOR-WURK) a program in which people in areas struck by disasters are paid each day by aid organizations to do a job

compassion (kuhm-PASH-uhn) sympathy for someone's misfortune; concern

debris (duh-BREE) scattered pieces of something that has been wrecked or destroyed

desperate (DESS-pur-it) feeling hopeless; willing to do anything to fix an urgent situation

Doctors Without Borders (DOK-turz with-OUT BOR-durz) an international organization that provides medical aid to people in areas affected by disaster or war

donations (doh-NAY-shuhnz) money that is given to help a good cause

earthquake (URTH-*kwayk*) shaking of the ground caused by the moving of Earth's outer layer

economy (i-KON-uh-mee) financial activity; includes all activities to create and spend wealth that occur in a particular place such as a city or country

evacuated (i-VAK-yoo-*ate*-id) moved away from an area that is dangerous

fund-raiser (FUHND-*ray*-zur) an event held to collect money for a charity or good cause

humongous (hyoo-MUHNG-*uhss*) huge

imported (im-PORT-id) brought from one country into another

international (*in*-tur-NASH-uh-nuhl) having to do with countries around the world

paramedics (*pa*-ruh-MED-iks) medical workers who ride in ambulances and give life-saving first aid

radar (RAY-dar) a tool that can find the location of an object by sending out radio waves

Richter scale (RIHK-tuhr SKALE) a number system used to indicate the strength of earthquakes; the higher the number, the more powerful the earthquake

rubble (RUHB-uhl) broken pieces of rock, brick, and other building materials

survivors (sur-VYE-vurz) people who live through a disaster or horrible event

tourism (TOOR-iz-uhm) the practice of traveling and visiting places for fun

victims (VIK-tuhmz) people who are hurt, injured, or killed by a person or event

volunteering (*vol*-uhn-TIHR-ing) doing a job without pay to help others

People beg for food and water outside a supermarket in Port-au-Prince Monday.

Bibliography

Editors of *Time*. *Haiti: Tragedy and Hope.* Des Moines, IA: Time (2010).

Figueroa, Laura. "American Who Lost Leg in Haiti Earthquake Returns a Good Deed." *The Miami Herald* (February 4, 2010).

Luhnow, David, and Ianthe Jeanne Dugan. "Haiti Quake Damage in Billions." *The Wall Street Journal* (February 17, 2010).

Romero, Simon. "Haiti Lies in Ruins; Grim Search for Untold Dead." *The New York Times* (January 13, 2010).

Read More

Reingold, Adam. *Leveled by an Earthquake!* New York: Bearport (2010).

Temple, Bob. *Haiti.* Broomall, PA: Mason Crest (2009).

Than, Ker. *Earthquakes.* Danbury, CT: Children's Press (2009).

Torres, John A. *Meet Our New Student from Haiti.* Hockessin, DE: Mitchell Lane (2008).

Learn More Online

To learn more about the earthquake in Haiti and ways to help disaster survivors around the world, visit **www.bearportpublishing.com/CodeRed**

Index

About the Author

Miriam Aronin is a writer and editor. She also enjoys dancing, knitting, and volunteering. She donated part of the money she earned from writing this book to an organization that provides earthquake relief in Haiti.